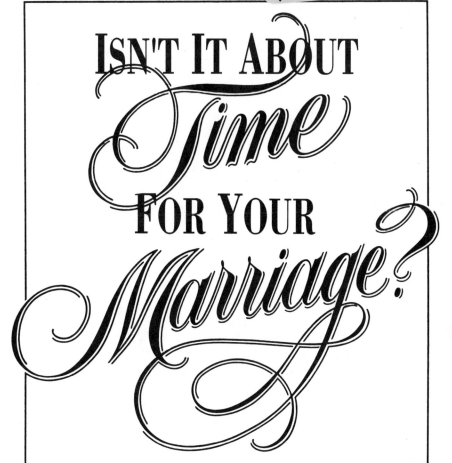

ISN'T IT ABOUT *Time* FOR YOUR *Marriage?*

MANAGEMENT PRINCIPLES TO STRENGTHEN YOUR RELATIONSHIP

BRYCE J. WINKEL, ED. D.
BARBARA A. WINKEL

ISBN 0-9630836-0-0

Library of Congress Catalog Card Number: 91-91177

First printing, Nov. 1991

Cover design by Rebecca Springer

Winco Publishing Company
2465 NW 145th Ave.
Beaverton, OR 97006

Printed in the United States of America

10 9 8 7 6 5 4 3 2 1

Dedication

To our parents: John and Rhoda Winkel, and Bryant Alfred and Afton Alder—You provided us with examples of dedication and security in marriage;

To our children: Richard, Bryan, Diana, Kristen, and John;

And to each other: May we in love and harmony reach our family goals.

TABLE OF CONTENTS

Acknowledgements

We extend appreciation and gratitude to the following people for their work and support:

Dick Winwood: You introduced us to the world of formal time management.

Norm Rose: You unselfishly provided word processing equipment, printing expertise, personal time and encouragement.

Louise R. Shaw, Jim Deming, Kay Zimmerman, Jim Alder, Diane Rose, Lisa Mosman and Thea Rhiannon: You provided valuable insights, critique and editing, which added much to the original manuscripts.

Berdell Moffett: You enthusiastically and lovingly took us on as a special project. Your expertise in publishing saved us years and made this book a reality.

Rebecca Springer and Ralph Bentley: Your artistic talents and intuition provided the cover design and typesetting.

Atesons Publishing: Thank you for allowing us to use selected quotations from the *Richard Evans' Quote Book.*

Forward

As a practicing physician, I regularly counsel patients who are experiencing marital problems.

Isn't It About Time For Your Marriage? embodies practical, straightforward and motivational advice to strengthen one's marriage. The authors' common-sense ideas, presented with warmth and humor, will aid those having marital struggles or will enhance the already successful marriage.

Success in marriage does not happen by chance, but rather is the result of couples carefully utilizing their time and setting priorities. I encourage all to read this book and apply its principles. The quality of marriages will improve, and couples will experience the profound joy that comes from a more harmonious family life.

Donald G. Bair, M.D.

INTRODUCTION

Have you ever thought, "I really ought to spend more time improving my marriage?" Due to the many demands and urgencies of life, it seems that the things that are most important to us often receive little of our time and attention.

For the past four years, Bryce has taught time management seminars. During this time, we have learned much that pertains to "time management in marriage." In fact, participants who attend Bryce's seminars often lament the fact that their spouses are not sharing the seminar experience with them.

Marriage could be considered the great American pastime. About 90 percent of us marry. Although statistics indicate that about half of all marriages end in divorce, about 80 percent of those who divorce remarry, most of them within three years. According to *The 1990 World Almanac,* the divorce rate increased dramatically between the years 1900 and 1980. The divorce rate has fallen slightly, however, during the decade of the 1980's. Perhaps we are seeing a beginning decline in divorce and a renewed commitment to making marriages successful.

We feel we have something of value to share with other married couples. We have been married for nineteen years. We have five children. (Two of them are normal, three of them are teenagers.) Bryce's salary has come mainly from school teaching, so we can relate to the budget challenges faced by most married couples. Bryce was raised in a farming community with a population of 4,000 and a high school of 400 students. Barbara is from a large metropolitan city where more than 2,000 students attended her high school. From these divergent backgrounds, we have worked and struggled to build a solid marriage relationship.

We believe in marriage. We share a strong commitment to each other and to our marriage. However, our marriage is not without its challenges. Like most of you, we came into our marriage relationship from different backgrounds and have different personality styles. We have learned that these differences can be strengths, as long as we share the same marriage values and goals. We recently completed our own MAP (Marriage Advancement Plan). We are aware of some of the difficulties—as well as the great potential benefits—of going through this process. It is our goal to share this MAP-building process with you. We assume that you, our readers, have some basic time management skills. If words such as planning, prioritizing, goal setting, "to do lists," etc. are unfamiliar to you, we suggest you read *How To Get Control of Your Time and Your Life* by Alan Lakein.

We believe that improving your marriage can also be compared to the principles involved in losing weight. The best weight loss techniques do not include crash dieting and constant fretting and weighing. Instead, success occurs when one practices correct nutrition principles and maintains a regular exercise program.

Applying the same logic, we suggest that you forget about constantly monitoring, worrying and questioning. ("Are we happily married yet?") It is our experience that you cannot force marital bliss. Simply learn and practice correct marriage principles. The natural result will be a happier, more enjoyable marriage relationship.

All we ask is that you read this book, complete your MAP, apply the principles for at least one month, and evaluate the results.

After all, isn't it about time for your marriage?

CHAPTER 1

Is Your Marriage Worth the Investment?

Marriage is at all times, in every culture and under the widest circumstances, one of the supreme tests of human character.
—*Hugh B. Brown*

Have you ever thrown something away only to realize later, to your dismay, that it was of value? When Bryce was a young boy, he collected baseball cards. Over the years of his youth, he purchased thousands of cards. As he got older, he lost interest or "outgrew" baseball card collecting, and one day he sold all his baseball cards to a friend for one dollar. If he had kept every baseball card he'd ever owned, they would now be worth many thousands of dollars.

We observe that marriage can be like this experience. Sometimes we don't appreciate what we have until we've lost it.

Is Divorce the Answer?

As with everything in which we invest our time, effort, and money, we must ask the question, "Is marriage worth what it costs?" A successful marriage requires hard work. Many divorcees come to realize that despite the challenges experienced during marriage, divorce is worse. They conclude that "knowing what I know now, yes, we could have made our marriage work." A great many couples who thought divorce would lead to increased peace and happiness now speak of splitting possessions, being uprooted from their homes, and seeing their family unit destroyed, often with their children becoming scapegoats.

Can Marriage Affect Your Health?

Much has been written recently to show that marriage is good for your health. Research has shown that both married men and married women have lower anxiety and depression than unmarried people. Evidence continues to mount linking better health to marriage and family life. In a recent "Social Science and Medicine" article, Catherine Riessman and Naomi Gerstel wrote: "One of the most consistent observations in health research is that married people enjoy better health than those of other marital statuses."

Confirming a long-held theory, a comprehensive study of death rates as far back as 1940 in sixteen industrial countries concluded that married people live longer than unmarried people. The death rates for unmarried men were generally twice as high as for married men, while the average death rate for unmarried women was one-and-one-half times that of married women. Divorced people, especially men, had the highest death rates. One explanation offered for the different rates is that people with partners to share their lives are better able to cope with stress in a rapidly changing world.

Marriage also exerts a deterrent effect on non-healthful activities, such as heavy drinking, risk-taking, drug usage and disorderly living. Harold Morowitz of Yale University researched the effects of marriage on health and concluded: "Being divorced and a non-smoker is slightly less dangerous than smoking a pack of cigarettes or more a day and staying married." He added facetiously, "If a man's marriage is driving him to heavy smoking, he has a delicate statistical decision to make."

What Causes Divorce?

Why do people divorce? Generally, we look for basic causes, such as infidelity, monetary disagreements, alcoholism or physical abuse. Researchers, however, are beginning to think these may be symptoms, not causes. Judith Wallerstein, co-author of *Surviving the Breakup,* testified in 1983 before a Senate subcommittee hearing on broken families. She said that infidelity was a prime cause for divorce in fewer than one-third of the divorces she studied. The central complaints were that spouses felt unloved, unappreciated and lonely in marriage. We feel that these complaints can be overcome, if couples are willing to invest the time and effort required to build a stable marriage.

There is a great movement today toward improving physical health. Many people have taken positive steps to improve their nutrition and exercise habits. A stable, happy marriage can also make a substantial contribution to overall physical and mental health.

The Rest of Your Life

Do you ever wonder how long you will live? It seems that the older we become, the more we value time and realize how quickly it is passing. What do you want to accomplish together during the rest of your married life? Most of us have dreams and wishes floating out somewhere in our future. You may dream of someday going on an exotic trip, building a new home, starting a family business or spending more time together. Your MAP (Marriage Advancement Plan) can help you make those dreams and wishes become reality.

As Bryce explained this concept at a recent time management seminar, a woman, who appeared to be about 45 years old, shared the following personal experience:

"For most of my married life, my husband and I didn't think we could afford to spend the money to do hardly anything. However, during the past three years, we've traveled to Hawaii and Europe. We also bought a 25-foot boat, and we spend as much time on it together as we can."

Why do you think there was such a drastic change in their marriage and financial values? Her answer: "Three years ago, we discovered that my husband has a terminal illness."

Do you realize that we all have a terminal illness? It's called simply "death." Although we may not know exactly when we will die, the certain reality of death should provide the urgency we need to seriously consider how we can make our dreams and wishes become reality.

This woman's story emphasizes the importance of goal setting. We are all acquainted with someone who is waiting to travel, or waiting to spend time together, or waiting to build a happy marriage—waiting until they retire, or when the business takes off, or when the kids are raised. That future may never come. **We ought to plan our lives and set our goals so as to live each day to its fullest.**

Isn't it about time for your marriage?

CHAPTER 2

The Challenge of Marriage

Marriage: The best method ever devised for becoming acquainted.
—Arnold Glasow

Although it appears that marriage has a positive effect on health, it is obvious that no marriage is free from problems. We are reminded of the young bride who said to her mother on her wedding day, "I'm the happiest girl in the world because I've come to the end of all my troubles." The wise mother answered, "Yes dear, you just don't know which end."

In marriage, there are frequent disagreements to work out and adjustments to make. We believe, however, that the health, peace and compatability that result from a strong marriage commitment are worth working for.

In *The Road Less Traveled,* Dr. Scott Peck suggests that to have a constructive marriage, the partners must regularly and routinely attend to each other and their relationship, no matter how they feel. He contends that all couples, sooner or later, fall out of love, and it is when the "honeymoon is over" that the opportunity for genuine love begins. It is when the spouses don't always want to be together that their love really begins to be tested. The person who truly loves his spouse does so because he has decided to love. This person loves whether or not the loving feelings of early marriage are present. **Genuine love is, therefore, a function of our decisions, not our conditions.**

A modern philosopher observed that there seems to be a general superstition among thousands of young people that marriage is an ideal situation where an eternally young and handsome husband comes home each night to an eternally young and beautiful wife who, of course, has a lovely candlelight dinner prepared which will be eaten in a spotless, debt-free home. When the reality of married life sets in, with the appearance of boredom, bills, and babies, the divorce courts are crammed. Anyone who imagines that married life will always be bliss is going to waste a lot of time feeling disappointed and cheated.

Our experience is that success in marriage is achieved through the conscientious attention to simple details that help overcome discouragement and disappointment. Bryce puts it this way: When Barbara gives me a relaxing bedtime backrub, even though she's as tired as I am, or when I offer to do the dishes after Barbara's hectic day with the children—these are the kinds of small but unselfish acts of love and consideration that help to strengthen a relationship and build bonds of love and appreciation.

We learn to love those things that are important to us. With love comes the risk of loss or rejection. If you are not willing to risk some pain, then you will never experience the joy of marriage and family relationships—the very relationships that give life meaning.

Is There Something Wrong with Your Spouse?

When something goes wrong with our marriage, we often conclude that the problem is a character defect in our spouse. We reach this conclusion because we assume that our spouse should see things the same way we do. In reality, it is in these very differences that the real strength in a relationship can be found!

Confrontations

Closeness thrives best in an atmosphere where partners show mutual respect, and where they accept and even value differences. Frequent confrontations, which often lead to stalemates or the holding of grudges, can destroy the intimacy and communication that are critical to building a lasting relationship. We shouldn't expect total compatability. **We should, however, expect the loyalty and commitment necessary to deal constructively with differences.**

Confrontations can cause a couple to grow apart. One or both of the partners may then attempt to cope with the empty marriage by filling themselves with food, work, an extra-marital affair, television, romance novels, alcohol, drugs or other such escape activities. These approaches do nothing to improve the marriage relationship.

The Strength in Differences

The physical differences between men and women are obvious and natural. These physical differences, of course, are what make it possible for us to create new life. Men and women also have emotional, mental and social differences. We believe that the emotional, mental and social differences between spouses can also create new and fulfilling forms of life in their marriage.

At our house, we often see and react to things differently. During the early years of our marriage, these differences created some problems. We both on occasion wondered, "Why can't you be more like me?" or "Why can't you see things like I do?" For example, even our honeymoon expectations were different. Barbara, the romanticist, envisioned an exotic trip. Bryce, the pragmatist, envisioned a less-expensive trip whereby we could save money and begin to set up our household. Barbara likes movies. Bryce thinks most movies are a waste of time and money. Bryce likes to watch football games on TV. Barbara thinks football is a waste of time. Does this sound anything like your marriage? Most of us wrestle with the age-old question expressed by Henry Higgins in *My Fair Lady:* "Why can't a woman be more like a man?" and vice versa. **How we react to and utilize these differences becomes a real key to marriage success.**

Over the years, we have come to appreciate the benefits and added dimension of two heads being better than one. This book is a direct result of our applying our differences in a constructive way. Bryce is "conceptual," whereas Barbara is more detail-oriented. Bryce did most of the actual writing of this book. As he created the ideas for each chapter, he gave them to Barbara in rather rough form. She then typed, edited and punctuated, adding her own ideas here and there, until the manuscript was polished and readable. We have enjoyed working together and appreciate each other's contributions. We realize that the only way we could have written this book was as a "team."

In corporate seminars, Bryce often teaches, "If everyone who works here were exactly like you, you wouldn't be needed." The same is true in marriage. Learn to respect and value your spouse's opinions and perspectives, especially if they are different from your own.

The 4 x 4 Marriage Approach

Have you ever experienced four-wheel drive? As a young farm boy and as a camper and hunter, Bryce often drove a pickup truck on muddy, slick, even dangerous roads. There were times when his vehicle became really stuck. It seemed impossible to go further. At times like this, he locked in the front wheel hubs and shifted the truck transmission into four-wheel drive. The results always seemed miraculous. With the rear wheels pushing and the front wheels pulling, the resulting cooperation multiplied the contribution of each wheel. Traction was regained and progress was made, despite the road conditions.

There are many opportunities to apply this four-wheel drive concept in marriage. When your marriage road becomes slick and muddy—maybe even dangerous, pull and push together, not separately or apart. Your traction will be regained, and you will begin to progress once again. Eventually, the storm will pass and the road ahead will improve.

Overcommitment

We are all limited in our time and energy. We feel that the real reason marriage problems arise is because our marriage is in competition with our jobs, our children, our hobbies, our house, etc. The premise of this book is that marriage should rank as one of our very highest priorities.

We believe that the major problem in many marriages today is overcommitment to interests and activities outside of marriage. We feel this overcommitment is a form of marital suicide. We all want to succeed in life. We want to do better and be better at our jobs, our hobbies, our investments, and as parents—but can any other success truly compensate for failure in our marriage? Overinvolvement in so many activities leads to physical and mental exhaustion. **If you are too tired to do anything together, you have no advantage over couples who don't *want* to do anything together.**

To summarize these ideas, we share this humorous thought: "To prove his love for her, he swam the deepest river, crossed the widest desert and climbed the highest mountain. She divorced him. He was never home."

Limiting Commitments

What can be done to limit our involvement in outside activities? In our back yard, we have about a dozen fruit trees. Each winter, Bryce prunes many of the branches. As he does so, he undoubtedly cuts off many branches that could bear fruit. But the act of cutting and pruning is the very process that allows the remaining branches to flower and produce larger, better-quality fruit.

In a similar way, life offers many opportunities for our talents and interests to branch out. The wise person prioritizes his life and prunes some of his lower-priority interests. This might mean pruning some interests that are worthwhile and enjoyable. One of our favorite sayings is, "You can do anything you want, but you cannot do everything." We must learn to "just say no" to some lower-priority requests for our time. Remember to smile when saying "no," because in reality, you are saying "yes" to something else of higher priority.

Begin to prune some things that compete with your marriage. We know it will be difficult. We suggest that you approach it with the same discipline you use to follow a healthy diet. You choose not to eat or drink certain things because you know they're not good for your body. Likewise, cut certain activities from your life because they're in competition with your marriage, and not as important. You may have convinced yourself that you "have to" work late, or play golf, or attend professional organizations, or be on the PTA board, etc. But the truth is, **you choose to do these things, and you have the same freedom to choose not to do them.** We must accept responsibility for our choices. Change occurs when there is confrontation. Therefore, look those outside commitments squarely in the eye. Compare the time you invest in them vs. the same amount of time invested in your marriage. Do they have the potential to bring you the same long-term return? If not, prune away!

When we love and value something, we spend time on it. Despite our lip service, we can tell what we truly value by how much time we invest in it. For example, a person who "loves" to golf, or garden, or fish, or read, somehow "makes the time" to do these things. Therefore, **if you truly value your marriage, you will somehow create the time to nurture your relationship.**

Visualization Exercise: Ninety-year-old Memories

Before we consider some ideas that will help you improve your marriage relationship, we would like you to visualize the following:

Imagine that you are 90 years old. You are sitting in a very comfortable chair. You are reminiscing about your life. At 90 years of age, most of what you have left are your memories. Slowly read, ponder and answer the following questions:

What do you want to remember about your married life?

What positive experiences do you remember?

Where did you and your spouse vacation?

How was your sexual relationship?

How did you spend your discretionary money?

Would you include your spouse high on your list of best friends?

Were you happy together?

Did you laugh often together?

Were you complimentary to each other?

How did you handle differences of opinion?

What was unique about your relationship?

How did you express your love for each other?

You may want to discuss this experience as a couple.

As Samuel Johnson said, "The future is bought with the present." Are you presently building the marriage memories that your mind just described? What can you do **now** to create the marriage memories that you want to look back on when you are 90 years old?

What are the Highest Priorities of my Life?

Bryce recalls hearing an unforgettable story that helps us consider our highest priorities:

A pilot alone in a small two-engine plane radioed an East coast air traffic controller with the following report: "When I left my home in the Midwest this morning, it was a beautiful day for flying. After several hours, I turned on my autopilot and went to sleep. Now I'm over water. I don't know how far I am from land, and I have only enough fuel to last for fifteen minutes." Air traffic controllers checked bearings and concluded that the pilot was about an hour from land over the Atlantic Ocean. The pilot was advised to head back toward land, and he was told that rescue planes and boats were on the way. Fearing the worst, the pilot radioed this message to the tower: "Tell my wife and children that I love them and that I'm very sorry." This was his final communication. He was never heard from again.

What do you suppose that pilot thought about for the last ten minutes of his life? We doubt he was concerned about a Monday morning business meeting, whether he should install a new phone system, whether to hold or sell a certain investment, or any of a hundred other typical daily concerns.

Employment is an example of an important aspect of our life. However, can you imagine anyone, on his deathbed, wishing he had spent more of his life at work?

Alan Lakein, a renowned time management consultant, suggests that we ask ourselves this question: "If I knew I would be struck dead by lightning six months from today, how would I live my life until then?" The purpose of this question is to help us determine if we are presently doing the things that are of highest priority to us.

Is your marriage relationship among the highest priorities of your life? Are you conscientiously and regularly working on your marriage relationship? Isn't it about time you do?

CHAPTER 3

The Art of Communication

Winning a love once is not enough. Keep rewinning it... In the last analysis, it's up to you to save your marriage.
—Hubert S. Howe

Volumes have been written suggesting ways in which couples can improve their marriages. It is our observation that too much of education is about knowing and not enough about doing. Our goal is to help you develop a MAP (Marriage Advancement Plan) that will provide direction and instructions for your "doing."

Chapters 3 and 4 contain suggestions for enhancing your marriage. The ideas come from our research, personal experiences and observations of other married couples. The ideas presented will probably not be new or revolutionary. It seems that everything has already been said that needs to be said—but since no one was listening, it needs to be said again. The common sense, golden rule, "Treat others as you would like to be treated," forms the basis for most personal relationship principles.

As you read each idea presented in this chapter, ask yourself: To what extent is this principle being applied in our marriage? Would our marriage relationship improve if we did this better or more often? Write your answers and feelings on the note pages at the back of this book. The notes you make will be helpful as you develop your MAP.

Look for the Positive

Marriage requires the maturity to know that because we aren't perfect people, our marriage will not be perfect. Marriage is, in fact, an uncompromising commitment to an imperfect person. Things seldom go exactly as we want. Couples who are happily married, however, will tend to focus on what they like about each other instead of what they don't like. If you look for and accentuate your spouse's positive qualities, his or her weaknesses will be viewed only as minor irritations. Constant fault-finding is guaranteed to drive love out of your marriage, so **look for the positive.**

Your courtship, like ours, was undoubtedly characterized by a tremendous commitment to each other. During courtship, couples practically live for each other. They are very concerned about their personal appearance, being on time, spending time together, etc. Bryce's father was a farmer with a good sense of humor. After we had dated for about a year and were spending a great deal of time together, he told Bryce, "Why don't you just marry that little girl so you can forget about her?" His statement, given in jest, has a lot of truth to it. In actuality, that is what often happens.

Most courtship experiences and conversations revolve around how wonderful each partner is. After we're married, however, we must deal with jobs, bills, house maintenance, children, etc. We often lose sight of what attracted us to each other in the first place. For example, after the honeymoon is over, couples often go their own way, pursuing careers, hobbies and old friends to the exclusion of the marriage commitment, assuming that their relationship will somehow take care of itself "now that we're married."

Visualization Exercise: Rekindle Positive Feelings

To help you rekindle those positive feelings, please take part in this visualization exercise. You will need at least ten minutes of quiet, uninterrupted time. Make yourself comfortable, although you may want to write down some of your ideas and feelings.

Close your eyes and relax. Let your mind wander back to the months and weeks prior to your wedding. Picture your fiancee. Rekindle the feelings you had for your soon-to-be spouse. Contemplate and list on a piece of paper several of the qualities that first attracted you to each other and led to your decision to spend the rest of your life with this person. What activities did you do together that created those positive feelings? Remember some of your firsts: first date, first kiss, first visit to his/her home. What made you proud to be with him/her? What kinds of things did you enjoy doing for each other? What things made you laugh together? What pet words or phrases were unique to your relationship? How and where did you propose? When you were separated, what were some of the warm, happy thoughts you had about your sweetheart?

After completing this visualization exercise, share and discuss your list and feelings with each other.

Make Time for Communication

Although life's circumstances have changed from the early days of your courtship and marriage, you can rekindle many of the earlier feelings. This can be done, in part, by looking for and accentuating the positive qualities of your spouse. Happy couples are constantly talking to each other about all aspects of their lives. If you want to grow closer, don't wait until you have time to talk—make time. Yes, it takes time to communicate, but it takes more time to correct mistakes caused by a lack of communication. Set aside time every day to talk.

Go for a daily 15-20 minute walk together. Have a special treat after dinner or visit about things after the children are in bed. Make time to become "best friends" again.

Discuss and work out your marriage problems together rather than succumbing to the temptation of turning to a friend. Friends can sympathize and agree with you, but your friend can only speculate as to why your spouse has done this or that. Only through open communication between you and your spouse can you ever hope to resolve a problem.

Miscommunication

A judge was interviewing a woman regarding her upcoming divorce, and inquired: "What are the grounds for your divorce?" She answered, "About three acres with a nice home in the middle of the property."

"No," he said, "I mean what is the foundation?"

"It's made of brick and concrete."

"I mean, what are your relations?"

"I have a cousin, an aunt and an uncle, and so do my husband's parents."

He tried again. "Is there infidelity in your marriage?"

"Yes, we have two stereo sets."

"Lady, does your husband ever beat you up?"

"Yes," she replied. "He gets up earlier than I do most mornings."

The frustrated judge finally asked, "Lady, why do you want a divorce?" She answered, "Oh, I've never wanted a divorce.

My husband wants a divorce. He says he can't communicate with me."

Conversational Differences

Every human relationship requires communication. Without it, there could be no relationship. The more intimate a relationship is, the more important communication becomes. Good communication skills are always found within strong marriage relationships.

We all have a longing to be heard—but not **merely** to be heard. We want to be understood as well. But as we have all experienced on occasion, when men and women communicate, misunderstandings can arise and dissatisfactions sometimes occur. As Bill Cosby says in *Love and Marriage,* "Just when you think you know all there is to know about your mate, something pops up to bewilder you, for men and women belong to a different species and communication between them is a science still in its infancy."

Deborah Tannen explains this dilemma well in her recent best-seller, *You Just Don't Understand: Men and Women in Conversation.* She writes that while men and women may use the same words, they use conversation differently. Men and women have basic differences in communication patterns and styles, and misunderstandings often arise because the styles are so different.

For example, Tannen describes one style difference as Reporting vs. Rapport. Men talk to convey information, and they tend to focus on the information being talked about. Women often talk to connect with others, and they are more comfortable with give and take. A woman, therefore, may feel that a man is lecturing.

Another example is described as Solution vs. Sharing. Men offer solutions, while women want to share their feelings. Women often talk about problems for a sense of empathy and knowing they're not alone. Men can mistake these discussions as literal requests for advice and offer solutions. Women then are likely to feel three frustrations: the discussion is cut short, she shouldn't even be talking about it because it's so easily fixed, and she feels put down. When couples ask for and offer clarification ("Do you want advice—or do you just need me to listen?"), we begin to ease some of the effects of our conversational differences.

Once people realize that their partners have different conversational styles, they are inclined to accept differences without blaming themselves, their partners or their relationship. Understanding the other person's way of talking is a giant leap across the communication gap between men and women, and a giant step toward opening lines of communication.

Perceptions

Two important things can be revealed through open communication: One, your spouse's behavior makes perfectly good sense when you understand his/her perception, and two, your personal perception is not necessarily the only or the correct perception. We often completely misinterpret what our spouse says or does simply because we don't know the background and past experiences that have formed his or her perceptions. **A large part of marriage problem-solving is to see your spouse's point of view.**

One winter, early in our marriage, we were living in an area that was experiencing a severe cold spell. Barbara tells it this way: We had a toddler and a new baby at that time, and I spent most of my days at home, dealing with the challenges of young motherhood and cabin fever. For several mornings, as Bryce left for work, he asked me to please keep the living room drapes closed during the day. I remember feeling resentful about his request because I felt I needed to see the sun and the outside world to help me maintain my sanity. I finally expressed my frustrations to Bryce and why I wanted to keep the drapes open. He then explained the reason for his request. He was concerned about the high cost of heating our home that season, and he felt the insulation provided by closing the thick drapes would help reduce these costs. Once we communicated about the problem and Bryce understood my feelings about the situation, he encouraged me to leave the drapes open.

It is important to understand what your spouse really wants. You may try hard to please, only to be frustrated because you missed the target.

Too often we listen only so that we can give our opinion, response or rebuttal. Learn to listen intently to understand and empathize with your spouse. Try to see things from his or her perspective.

Never Assume Anything

Often problems arise because we assume we know what is right, or we assume we know how our spouse feels or should feel. We strongly suggest, based on observation and some personal experience, that you **never assume anything** regarding your marriage relationship.

The story is told of a husband and wife dressing to go out to a dinner party. The wife asked her husband to please zip up her dress. He was in a rather playful mood, so he grabbed the zipper and gave it two or three quick up-and-down jerks. This caused the zipper to become stuck in the wife's slip. Try as he would, he could not free the zipper. He finally resorted to using a pair of scissors to cut the zipper out of the slip, a process that ruined both the dress and the slip. Needless to say, the wife was not happy.

About a week later, as she returned home from an errand and walked up the driveway, she noticed her husband's legs sticking out from under their car. She thought, "Great! This is my chance to give him a dose of his own medicine." She reached down, grabbed the zipper attached to the fly of his pants, and gave it a couple of quick up-and-down jerks. This caught him by surprise. His reaction was rapid, including a "clunk" as he banged his head on the car's oil pan.

She continued up the driveway and through the front door of their home, feeling satisfied that she had taught him a valuable lesson. She walked into the kitchen, and there, to her surprise, stood her husband by the kitchen sink. She recovered enough from her shock to ask, "Dear, who's that lying underneath our car?" His reply: "Oh, that's our neighbor Fred. He's helping me do a little repair work."

This story is both humorous and embarrassing. It does, however, illustrate the trouble you can get into when you assume something. Learn to ask questions rather than assume you know all the facts about a certain situation. Remember, we tend to see the world through the eyes of our own experience. When communicating, learn to say, "This is the way I see it" rather than "This is the way it is."

Be Positive

For the most part, make your communication positive. Express love by both word and action. Some spouses, particularly husbands, have trouble showing affection and saying gentle and loving things. It isn't right for your spouse to have to guess whether or not you love him/her. Simple, sincere, spontaneous compliments add great strength to a relationship. This sounds easy to do, yet we are often better at praising other people than we are at complimenting our spouse. Frequently we think nice things about our spouse, but neglect to say them. Even if you "assume" your spouse knows how you feel, express it again!

Here is an example from Barbara's experience: One of the qualities I appreciate in Bryce is his ability to express appreciation for even the simplest things. Bryce grew up in a home where expressing thanks was a common occurrence. I noticed and was impressed with this characteristic early in our relationship. For example, when I visited his home before we were married, I noticed the sincere and enthusiastic way in which each person, during family dinners, told their mother how much they enjoyed the meal. They did this no matter what was served (although it was always delicious!) because they appreciated the skilled and loving hands that had prepared it.

I am grateful that this important training, learned in his youth, continues into married life. Many times, Bryce's simple but sincere expressions of appreciation have been real day-brighteners to me. We are making an effort to continue this "gratitude attitude" in our family.

Along with expressing appreciation goes accepting compliments graciously. If your spouse compliments the way you look, don't contradict him/her by pointing out that you really ought to lose a few pounds, or you wish you had a different hair style, etc. When your spouse praises you, accept the compliment graciously and say "thank you." Look for opportunities to return the compliment.

Could you strengthen your marriage relationship by communicating more often and more positively?

CHAPTER 4

A Small Investment Earns a Great Return

If a man gets wise, he gets rich, an' if he gets rich, he gets foolish, or his wife does. That's what keeps the money movin' around.
                                        —*Finley Peter Dunne*

Marriage and Money

For some couples, handling money comes easily. But for others, conflicts over finances can seem insurmountable. A recent American Bar Association statistic indicates that 89 percent of all divorces relate to money problems. And a recent Associated Press national survey concludes that money causes more arguments in American households than any other topic, and it is the leading cause of dissension in virtually all income groups. Thirty-seven percent of households reported that they had clashed about money during the preceding twelve months. A 1986 "Money Magazine" survey further concludes that nearly half of all Americans are dissatisfied with their finances, and more than a third of adults think fatter wallets would improve their sex lives.

A new marriage is very much like a corporate merger. Two people, usually with very different money-handling habits, are suddenly forced to combine those different methods to manage one source of funds and one household.

We believe that money management in a marriage should be on a partnership basis, with both parties having a voice in decision-making and policy-making. It is impossible to have love, peace and security when financial anxieties and bickering are prevalent.

From our study and observation, the size of a couple's income seems to have little bearing on the number and degree of financial problems. It appears that marriage tragedies are not caused simply by a lack of money, but rather by the mismanagement of personal finances. **Money management, therefore, should take precedence over money production.**

Money Talks

Our first suggestion is that marriage partners apply the communication techniques described in Chapter 3 to their financial dealings. If either spouse feels insecure or unsure about where the money is going, problems are sure to follow. On the other hand, if both know where the money is going, it doesn't matter who writes the checks. We rarely spend money without letting the other know for what it's being spent. This even includes minor purchases, which can add up quickly if not controlled. Discussing before buying also serves as a deterrent to impulse or emotional buying.

Communication makes it possible to reach a mutual decision. Serious problems result when one spouse arbitrarily announces, "No, you can't buy that." Another potential problem is the attitude of "This is my money. I'll spend it however I want." We feel that no matter which spouse earned the money, all the money should belong to both. This does not mean that each spouse could not have some discretionary money or petty cash to spend as he or she chooses. This can be discussed, decided and budgeted for—as a couple.

Many people enter marriage without having really learned the value of money. Before marriage, many of us are accustomed to having whatever we want, either because ease and luxury are furnished by our parents, or because ease and freedom are provided by a good job. While we are single, we have to meet only our own needs and desires. Pre-marriage financial situations can create a natural inclination to selfishness at worst or lack of financial self-discipline at best.

We need to develop lifestyle expectations based on the reality of our incomes. A professional marriage counselor lamented that he has talked to many couples who don't have enough money to meet their basic needs or begin a savings account, but who, nevertheless, go out and buy a boat. Some couples seem to try to take their minds off their financial troubles by going out to dinner and a movie every weekend! We know couples who charge money on their credit cards to take their two-week summer vacations. Many couples fritter away their money and then wonder where it went.

Financial Freedom

Budget has become a dirty word in some circles. The word conjures up negative feelings of restraint, cut-backs and discipline. We believe, however, that this very discipline is what leads eventually to financial freedom.

How much does a dress cost if the price is $90? Perhaps the question sounds foolish. The answer, however, is this: A $90 dress costs $90 plus everything else you could have purchased with that $90, had you not bought the dress. This principle is sometimes referred to as the "law of opportunity costs." Every day, as we make decisions regarding the use of our time or money, we are subject to this law.

You can tell much about a couple's marriage values by how they spend their money. Have you ever noticed a modest home with two fancy, expensive automobiles parked in the driveway? Do you know a couple with a large, expensive home with hardly any furniture? Or a family with a secure savings account but a modest lifestyle? Or a couple who frequently go out to movies, dinner (or other entertainment) or on expensive trips, while living in a rented apartment? All lifestyles represent financial choices based on what we value.

A realistic budget is no guarantee against financial problems. But without a budget, a couple is left to the mercy of easy credit, slick advertising and our own natural desires to consume, have and keep up with what our friends have. The no-budget approach often leads to a perpetual state of financial emergency—never sure why there isn't enough money to pay the bills. With a financial plan that is carefully followed, a couple at least has the security of knowing exactly where they stand financially.

We believe it is unwise to borrow money to purchase a depreciating asset. In other words, do not go into debt, with the exception of your home and possibly your car. When we save money in order to pay cash for something, the bank pays us interest while we're waiting. If we go into debt to make a purchase, we pay interest to the bank. Furthermore, it is our experience that when we've finally finished paying for something we're buying on time, it's old, used and maybe even worn out. Remember, except for food, shelter and necessary clothing, there's nothing we need so badly that we can't wait.

It's nice to own lots of "things," but we can do without them. What's really important is our marriage relationship. This attitude assures that financial problems will rarely be insurmountable. When financial setbacks do come, we can face them as a unified couple, refusing to be divided. Don't let money be a wedge between you and your spouse. The idea of having "enough money" may not be an amount as much as an attitude. **Perhaps we need to become more content with the things we have and less content with what we are.**

Variety

Variety can truly add spice to a marriage. Most of us exchange gifts on special occasions, such as Christmas, birthdays and anniversaries. These gifts can become expected and are often taken for granted. A gift that is given as a total surprise, however, carries an impact worth much more than the price of the gift.

We encourage you to surprise your spouse with an occasional gift for no other reason than "just because I love you." These gifts need not be expensive. In fact, small, sentimental gifts or gifts of "doing something enjoyable together" are often best. You might ask your spouse to help you create a gift list. Then you could add to this list as you become aware of new ideas. There are periods when life becomes extra hectic, leaving little time for marriage-building activities. During these times, you could refer to your gift list and bring your spouse a little gift as a reminder that you're still "in love" and looking forward to married life returning to normal.

A wife and mother of several small children commented recently that one of the nicest things her husband ever did for her was to arrange a weekend away for just the two of them. She added that it was a total surprise and that he had done all the planning, made the reservations and even arranged for a babysitter. How do you think she felt about her husband that weekend and for months to come? Such an act is a wise investment in your marriage.

Your Physical/Sexual Relationship

For the most part, the quality of a marriage is reflected in the quality of the sexual relationship. Paul Pearsall has authored an interesting book titled *Super Marital Sex—Loving For Life.* It has been dubbed the "sexless sex book." Our experiences and observations regarding sexual intimacy support what he describes in his book.

Have you ever heard someone make a comment regarding his or someone else's "sex life?" In reality, no one has a "sex life" any more than he or she has a "nutrition life" or a "sleep life." Sex is not something a couple does but a part of what they are. Sex is often taken out of context and made a totally separate part of marriage instead of an important part of the total marital relationship. We believe that marriage offers the best potential for fulfilling sexual expression because marriage provides a framework for the greatest emotional intimacy.

When people ask Pearsall how to have more and better orgasms, he responds, "Get next to each other emotionally. Find time to be together." He further states, "People don't put any time in their sex. If people spent as much time on their business as they do on their marriage, they'd be bankrupt."

Based on this approach to marital intimacy, almost everything described in this book is designed to improve your sexual relationship. Be best friends, give surprise gifts to each other, take walks together, communicate and express appreciation and affection. These can all make positive contributions to your marital intimacy.

In our busy lives, with time and energy in short supply, we can't afford to wait for a once-a-year vacation to restore sexual spice. Since we can rarely plan exotic, romantic retreats, we have to learn to be more romantic while doing the things we already do. Certain daily routines can be converted into intimate, playful opportunities.

Partners can dress or undress with a touch of flair. Women know that wearing clothing that makes them feel feminine and attractive contributes to feelings of intimacy. Opportunities for closeness can be created while watching TV together, driving in the car, showering, and many other such routine activities. Be open to the possibilities. Look for and create opportunities. Don't be too busy to be sexy. Intimacy is an attitude, not necessarily a physical setting.

Marriage and Baseball

A marital relationship can be compared to a baseball game. As we all know, the object of baseball is to advance the batter/runner from home plate (where he begins) to first base, second base, third base, and back to home.

A marital relationship begins at home plate. A couple advances to first base when they are kind and thoughtful and express courtesy toward one another. Second base is represented by unselfishness, such as sharing, forgiving and truly enjoying each other's company and friendship, with an increase in physical closeness. A couple can advance to third base when they have reached a level of trust, honesty and emotional intimacy, feeling safe with each other. It is only after passing each of these bases that a couple may continue on to home plate, which is represented by complete and total sexual intimacy. Some partners want to hit a home run without passing the rest of the bases. This is an infraction of the rules of both baseball and marriage.

Intimate Planning

Spouses often give each other time that is "left over" from the rest of the day. Plan to spend time together when you still have some energy left. Schedule time for love-making.

Couples express fear that scheduling sex might cause them to lose their spontaneity. It's a myth that the best sex is spontaneous. In our busy world, most couples are too busy to do anything spontaneously. Chances are that if you don't plan sex dates, you won't spend much intimate time together.

Planning can actually improve the experience. The "anticipation" also builds excitement. It creates time for mood-enhancing activities like hot-tubbing, snuggling by a warm fire or giving each other massages.

Think back to your dating and courtship days. Remember how you planned and anticipated as you prepared for a Friday night date, contemplating what to wear, where to go, etc? The same excitement can occur if you plan marital intimacy, allowing time for mental and physical preparations.

As you coordinate schedules during planning sessions, decide which evenings, mornings, etc. will be reserved for time together. Sex may or may not be a part of these times together. In either event, your general relationship will be strengthened. Remember the enjoyment and importance that the first, second and third bases have to a fulfilling marriage relationship.

Couples schedule most personal and family commitments. Why do we think sex will somehow just take care of itself? As with almost anything, love doesn't just "happen." Its success is based on proper planning and correct choices.

CHAPTER 5

Developing Your MAP
(Marriage Advancement Plan)

Map (noun): something that represents with a clarity; to plan in detail; to program or devise for the future.
—Webster's Dictionary

Nothing gives so much direction to a person's life as a sound set of principles.
—Ralph Waldo Emerson

Do you like to travel? Have you ever driven a car in an unfamiliar city far from home? Think back to the first time you attempted to drive in a large city such as San Francisco or Chicago. Did you just start driving, making random turns, hoping to arrive at your desired destination? Our guess is that you do what we do when driving in unfamiliar territory: ask for directions and obtain a map.

A map is a graphic portrayal of all or part of the earth. Maps help us travel efficiently from place to place. Recently, Bryce experienced that tenuous, lost feeling as he drove away from a busy airport, unsure of exactly where he was supposed to go, yet feeling an urgency to arrive soon. It occured to us that marriage can be similar to arriving in an unfamiliar city. Our formal educational system offers few classes that prepare us adequately for marriage. Marriage is a learn-as-you-go proposition, with a great deal of trial and error. Probably most of your preparation for marriage came from observing your parents. They may or may not have been good teachers or examples.

What we need for success in marriage are directions and an accurate, detailed map. The directions for marriage can be found in the numerous words written and spoken by qualified marriage counselors. We believe you can, by following their directions and your own hopes, desires and common sense, develop your own marriage road map.

The MAP we speak of is the **"Marriage Advancement Plan."** An example of this approach comes from the life of Benjamin Franklin. When Franklin was a young man, he wrote thirteen personal virtues or values that he wished to develop. He also wrote a short description or personal definition of each value. He recorded these values on a separate page in a little black book that he always carried with him. Here are a few value examples, as recorded in his autobiography:

"Industry: Lose no time; be always employed in something useful; cut off all unnecessary actions."

"Silence: Speak not but what may benefit others or yourself; avoid trifling conversation."

"Order: Let all your things have their places; let each part of your business have its time."

Each day, Franklin evaluated his progress by comparing his performance to his written value statements. These statements became the "road map" for his life. They provided him with goals and direction. At the age of 79, writing in his autobiography, Franklin recorded the following:

"I entered upon the execution of this plan for self-examination and continued it, with occasional intermissions, but I always carried my little book with me. And it may be well my posterity should be informed that to this little artifice [his book] with the blessing of God, their ancestor owed the constant felicity of his life down to this 79th year in which this is written. I hope, therefore, that some of my descendants may follow my example and reap the benefit."

These same principles can be applied to increase the stability, success and happiness of your marriage.

Building Your MAP

The physical setting for building your MAP is an important consideration, and is discussed in Chapter 6. More critical than the setting, however, is your commitment. It has been our experience that for your MAP to have the greatest effect, each spouse must have a strong commitment to achieve a successful marriage.

The steps to building your MAP are as follows:

1. Identify marriage value categories.

2. Write ideal behavior statements.

3. Prioritize.

4. Set long- and short-term goals.

5. Schedule and act.

We suggest that you finish reading this chapter, which will give you a good overview of the MAP-building process. Then, when you are ready to begin building your MAP, return to this section and follow the step-by-step process.

Step 1: Identify Marriage Value Categories

Anything that is important to you and/or your spouse qualifies as a "marriage value." Marriage value statements help us define and visualize our highest marriage hopes, dreams and goals. They embody the "ideal" picture of marriage we imagined during courtship. In fact, these marriage values form the basic reasons we got married in the first place.

The first step is to select general categories wherein you can identify and define your specific marriage values. The marriage values that we have written fall under the following general categories:

Children/Family

Extended Family

Financial

Intellectual/Educational

Personal Fulfillment

Physical

Social

Spiritual

Work/Job/Profession

We have listed these value categories alphabetically since order and priority are not important at this point. You may want to add or select other categories, such as cultural, hobbies, political, community service, humanitarian, etc., depending on your interests and involvement. See Appendix A for forms designed to help you complete Steps 1 and 2.

Step 2: Describe Ideal Behavior

After you have selected general value categories, write statements describing ideal behavior supporting each value. We have found it most beneficial to write these statements as affirmations. Affirmations help us visualize and measure our desired behavior. They are also positive, and they help us become emotionally involved in our commitments.

As we share a few of our own marriage values as examples, please remember that your values will most likely be different from ours, and that our values are written as affirmations (statements of ideal behavior), and we haven't mastered them yet.

MARRIAGE VALUES (Introductory Statements)

Our marriage will last forever.

We practice positive relationship skills.

We calendar, plan and read our values together each Sunday evening.

We make time to build our marriage relationship.

Social

We plan at least one date per week.

We are best friends.

We enjoy each other's company.

We look for and compliment each other's positive traits. We settle differences quickly and positively before they become problems.

Children/Family

Our family is an important consideration in every decision we make.

We are both involved in raising our children.

We discuss and agree on child-rearing policies.

We spend one-on-one time with each child.

Our children rank second in importance, after our marriage.

Intellectual

We ask for and respect each other's opinions.

We carefully limit personal and family television viewing time.

Physical

We express affection daily.

We encourage each other to get enough rest, relaxation and exercise.

Extended Family

We support each other's families.

We speak positively about our families, neighbors and friends—or not at all.

Personal Fulfillment

We support each other's involvement in community, church and other social activities.

Financial

We prepare and follow a family budget.

We agree before making major purchases.

We earn more than we spend.

We save for future known and unknown expenses.

We read our value statements each Sunday evening as part of our regularly scheduled marriage planning meeting. As we take turns reading a value, we ask such questions as, "Are we doing this?" "When can we do it next?" "Should we set a specific date and time?" We also try to read our marriage values individually at least one other time during the week.

Our marital relationship was strengthened as we labored together through this value identification process. We have designed many of our value statements to address specific marriage situations where we have had conflicts in the past. This proactive approach has helped us deal with potential relationship problems before they occur. As we read our value statements, not only are we planning future activities, but we reminisce about pleasant and successful activities already enjoyed. These memories give added incentive and desire for future relationship-building activities.

We have concluded our marriage values with the following statement: **We realize that our differences are strengths because we have the same marriage and family values.**

Our purpose in sharing a few of our marriage value statements is to give you some ideas. You may find our approach too detailed. Feel free to adapt these ideas to your personality and lifestyle. Much of the growth and benefit of this experience come as you share and struggle together to form value statements with which you both feel comfortable.

This value identification and definition process will probably take between one and three hours. You may want to type this first draft on a word processor, since during the first few months you will undoubtedly change some of your value statements as you refine them.

An example of this refining comes from Bryce's experience, when he wrote his personal values. One of his first-draft statements read: "I appreciate all that Barbara does for me." As you can see, this statement is general and unmeasurable. No one benefitted just because Bryce walked around being appreciative. Therefore, he changed that statement to read: "I show and express appreciation to Barbara for all she does for me." Now, as he reads this value, he asks himself, "So, when was the last time I expressed appreciation?" Or, "What have I done lately to show Barbara I appreciate her?" The more measurable the value statement, the greater the effect it can have on your marriage behavior.

What if...?

What if only one partner is interested in making a MAP? We recently taught a seminar to a group of young mothers. Several women complained of having "non-communicative" husbands. These women expressed enthusiasm for MAP-building but feared that their husbands would not likely participate.

We have a friend who, after reading this book, commented, "I have a wonderful marriage and a husband who is perfect for me, but I know without any doubt that he would not be interested in formulating a MAP."

If this sounds anything like your present situation, how can you apply these principles to your marriage?

We know that it is possible to work as an individual to strengthen your marriage. Planning weekend getaways, even if you won't write anything down, often creates opportunities to talk, share ideas and rekindle romance. One spouse could ask the other to talk about the calendar for the coming week and suggest a marriage-related date or two as the schedule permits. A spouse who rejects writing a MAP probably would not resist this more subtle approach.

Another friend, who felt her husband wasn't quite ready to build a MAP, shared the following idea with us. She wrote three or four marriage enhancement statements (affirmations) on 3x5 cards, which she taped to the bathroom mirror. Her husband's response was positive, and it provided a basis for communication. She changes the 3x5 cards every week, and her husband is appreciative of what she is doing. This simple adaptation of the MAP shows commitment to her marriage and her husband. It has made a positive impact on their relationship.

Words like constrain, force, compel and coerce have no application in successful marriage partnerships. Attempts to force your partner to build and implement a MAP will cause more problems than they will cure. However, simple MAP variations and application of any of the general principles described in this book can make positive contributions to any marital relationship.

Step 3: Prioritize Your Value Statements

After you have finished writing your value statements, spend a few minutes prioritizing them. This can be rather difficult, because most values are interrelated and dependent on each other. Nonetheless, it is a revealing and beneficial communication exercise to discuss and prioritize your marriage values.

For a road map to be useful, it must be drawn to scale. Likewise, your MAP must be drawn to scale or it will be inaccurate. Our personal opinions and perceptions can distort our MAPs unless we take time to prioritize our marriage value statements. To accurately prioritize, we must determine whether each value statement is a need, a want or a wish. Since husband and wife perceptions are often different, this can best be determined by an honest and open husband-wife discussion.

Here is an example from Bryce's perspective: Barbara and I have had open discussions on numerous occasions, not always in a formal setting. For example, if Barbara returned from a shopping trip bearing major purchases that I considered to be low-priority ("wish"—not "need") items, the ensuing discussion (generally calm and controlled) would help me realize that Barbara really did need or want the items in question, or it would help Barbara realize that the purchases were perhaps a little frivolous, given our present financial situation. Depending on the outcome of this discussion, some items would perhaps be returned for a refund or kept with the understanding that these purchases were neccessary. The important point is not whether we keep the items, but that we communicate about it. **Communication is the key in making a decision that builds the marital relationship.**

Marriage Constitution

This values exercise could be referred to as writing your "marriage constitution." Just as each law of the United States is measured against the United States Constitution, your marriage values become the standard by which you measure daily decisions as they relate to your marriage. We like to refer to the MAP-building process as a "one-time investment in your marriage." It is a small investment of time and energy that we feel will pay high daily dividends for the rest of your life.

An executive of a large corporation recently expressed amazement at the number of people who can't seem to control their own schedules. Several executives working under him had stated with pride that they had worked so hard during the past year that they hadn't taken any vacations. He responded rather disgustedly that it seemed ridiculous to be able to take responsibility for multi-million dollar projects, yet be unable to plan two weeks out of a year to have a fun vacation with their families. He concluded that to make the best possible use of your time, you have to first decide what's most important and then give it all you've got. In marriage, writing value statements helps you know what's most important, and setting goals helps you give it all you've got.

Step 4: Set Long- and Short-term Goals

All the beautiful sentiments in the world weigh less than a single lovely action.
                                   —*James Russell Lowell*

If your marriage **behavior** is in line with your marriage **value statements,** you will have an ideal marriage. In other words, if you are doing all the things you described in your value statements, you will have, by your own definition, an ideal marriage. If your behavior is not completely in line with your marriage value statements, then goal setting is the process by which you bring your values and behavior in line.

Goal-setting is also the process of bringing future events under our control. It is the process by which we move from, or expand, our comfort zones. Goal setting leads to behavior change. Your value statements will serve as a guide for your goals. In fact, some of your values, written as affirmations, may actually be goal statements.

Keys to Effective Goal Planning

We usually spend months or even years forming habits or finding our comfort zones. It is, therefore, generally difficult to leave or change a comfort zone. Procrastination hovers close by. A habit is much like a warm bed: It's a lot easier to get into than it is to get out of. Reaching a goal often requires us to break a habit. For example, it is easier to watch TV than it is to spend the time and exert the energy required to build a great marriage. Improvement will require effort. Are you willing to pay the price?

An important initial step toward achieving goals is writing them down, for an unwritten goal is no goal at all. We usually don't take long-term plans very seriously when we make only a mental commitment to them. In fact, we generally don't even remember our plans for more than a few minutes. This is one of the reasons that businesses require written contracts and not just verbal commitments. Written goals also give us a point of reference against which we can check our progress.

Time spent pondering plans and goals without a pen and paper in front of us falls under the category of good intentions, not goal setting. Remember, **an unwritten goal is merely a wish.** Are you working or wishing?

Goals should be written in such a way that the desired result is clearly defined. As you write, picture yourself accomplishing your goal. There is a "magic gravitation" that occurs when we write a goal, visualize ourselves accomplishing it, and then finally exert the effort to accomplish our goal.

Use the S.M.A.R.T. method to make your goal-setting more effective:

S - Specific

M - Measurable

A - Attainable

R - Realistic

T - Time-scheduled

There are several goal-setting forms at the back of Appendix A, beginning on page 88.

Each spouse should be committed to attaining the goal. Set high standards that require you to stretch, but do not be unreasonable.

Short-term Goals

When we write short-term or intermediate goals, we break down our long-range goals into "do-able" pieces. They give encouragement and reinforce our efforts to achieve our long-range goals. These intermediate steps should be specific and measurable. Most short-term goals can be completed as daily tasks. This leads us to the real purpose of our MAP, which is the literal "doing" to achieve our desired results.

Consider the following sample marriage goal:

Marriage value: Financial

Long-term Goal:

One year from today (January 2), we will be out of debt (except for house and car payments), and we will be saving at least $200 per month.

Short-term Goals:

1. We review our bank statement and budget by the 10th of each month. (Deadline: Jan. 10)

2. We have stopped using our credit cards. (Deadline: Jan. 2)

3. We pay an extra $200 per month on our credit card bill until it is totally paid off. (Deadline: May 1)

4. We will not purchase any new clothes for three months. (Deadline: Mar. 1)

5. We save $50 per month in a separate interest-earning savings account. (Deadline: Mar. 30)

6. Our summer vacation is planned to cost less than $375. (Deadline: May 20)

7. We save $100 per month. (Deadline: June 30)

8. Our Christmas expenses are less than $600 this year. (Deadline: Dec. 25)

9. We save $200 per month. (Deadline: Dec. 1)

This goal is illustrated in Appendix A on page 89.

Step 5: Schedule and Act

There is a certain amount of idealism in the value identification and goal-setting process we have just described. In reality, if we actually strengthen our marriage relationship, it will be because we are doing something positive today—actually right now! Measurable benefits rarely come from talking or reading about marriage improvement. Measurable benefits come because spouses begin to **say** nice things to each other. They **do** things for each other and with each other. They **show** or **demonstrate** love through their actions. **Can you see that love is not a noun? Love is an action verb.**

Isn't it about time to say, do, show, and demonstrate love in your marriage?

True Education Equals Behavior Change

Bryce grew up working on his father's turkey farm. The story is told of an adventuresome tom turkey who one day gathered all of his friends together. For several hours, he provided training and demonstrations that taught the turkeys how to fly. All day long, they experienced the exciting thrills and perspectives made available through flight. But later, after the class ended, all of the turkeys walked home.

For more than eighteen years, Bryce has been a professional educator. It is his observation that too often we fail to apply the principles and ideas that are taught. We've all attended classes and seminars, or read interesting ideas. These educational experiences make us aware of our weaknesses, and we often resolve to do better or be better. But generally, within a week or so, our resolve and motivation fade, and we end up having changed very little. Most of our New Year's resolutions fit this description.

It seems that many of us treat our marriage relationship the way we sometimes watch television. Even though the program isn't as good as we would like, we're too lazy to get up and change it.

Barbara also experiences this dilemma in her occupation as a dental hygienist. For example, most of her patients "know" they should be flossing their teeth daily, but not all of them actually do it. She diligently teaches them the benefits and advantages of flossing, and the proper technique, but still there are those who do not incorporate this habit into their daily routines.

We believe that in the truest sense of education, if your behavior does not change, you have not really learned anything. **Genuine learning equals behavior change.** Much of what is taught is interesting, motivational, and has value. Most educational experiences, however, lack a tool that could help us implement the desired behavior changes.

The Date Book Organizer

We believe that maintaining control and staying organized on a daily basis is best done with the use of a date book organizer. This becomes your application tool. Date book organizers come in various sizes, prices and degrees of complexity. For our general suggestions regarding a date book organizer, see Appendix B.

Marriage Rhythm

Not long ago, a friend asked Barbara to join her in playing a piano duet. Barbara has studied the piano for many years and is a skilled pianist. After the duet, Barbara noted that her friend kept starting and stopping unexpectedly, making it difficult for them to play together. In piano duets, dancing and marriage, it's difficult to know what to expect and how to react when you and your partner do not follow the same rhythm. We feel that creating your MAP together can help you in your quest to share the same rhythm.

This process of describing values and setting goals has had and continues to have a profound impact on our marriage relationship.

We're sure you know for yourself the thousands of daily marriage experiences and decisions that can test, strengthen, build, attack, or even destroy your love and commitment. We encourage you to invest in your present and future marital success by building your MAP.

CHAPTER 6

Keys to Making Your MAP Effective

For the acquirement of solid, uniform, steady virtue, nothing contributes more than daily, strict self-examination...joined with firm resolutions of amending what you find amiss.
—Benjamin Franklin

Planning

Planning is the process that transfers ideas from your MAP (which is the ideal) to your daily schedule (which is reality).

If you were the manager of a growing company, would you attempt to run your business without ever holding a meeting? Imagine a business without executive board meetings or employee staff meetings. Your marriage is somewhat like a mini-corporation. It consists of physical facilities management, budget and expenditure considerations, scheduling, communication, purchasing, transportation, insurance, etc. When was the last time you sat down with your spouse in an "executive board meeting?"

As mentioned earlier, we hold a planning meeting each Sunday evening. We review our upcoming schedules. We read our MAP to see which of our marriage values and goals can be accomplished during the coming week. We know that proper prior planning prevents pretty poor performance. In other words, **planning is the key to positive performance.**

Isn't is about time you, as a couple, started planning regularly?

Prioritizing

In our opinion, prioritizing is the single most important principle in life. Why do you work where you work? Why do you live where you live? Why did you marry the person you married? In almost every case, we have chosen to do the things we do because, at least at the time we made the decision, it represented what was most important to us, or it seemed to be the best choice we could make. Thus, we considered all of our options and selected the best or "highest priority" option. Time has been called "God's democracy" because everyone is given the same amount. The busiest person in the world has 24 hours a day. The person who has nothing to do also has 24 hours a day. The law of "supply and demand" has no effect on our personal time allotment. You may be very different from other people regarding most aspects of life, but you have as much time as the richest, most powerful, most beautiful person in the world. You should never say "I didn't have enough time" because, in fact, you had all the time there was. Applying this same logic, if you say, "I don't have time for my marriage," what you are saying in reality is "I value other things more than I value my marriage."

Time can be like money. If you spend your money to purchase one item, you lose the opportunity to spend that money on a different item. If you decide to spend your time doing one activity, you have also decided not to spend that time on any other activity. **Deciding which activity will bring us the greatest return on our time invested is the process of prioritizing.**

Urgency can be the great enemy of prioritizing. An urgent activity cries out for immediate attention. It says, "Do me now!"

We often say "yes" to the urgent requests made on our time by our work, our friends, our hobbies, our clubs, our churches, or our communities. Do you realize that each time you say "yes" to one activity, you also say "no" to everything else you could have done during that time?

Marriage enhancement activities, including dating, walking, planning, talking, loving, sharing, etc., are classified as "high value" but "low urgency" activities. As such, we seldom make time for them. The process of making time for your marriage is as follows:

1. Identify your highest marriage priorities by building your MAP.

2. Hold a weekly planning session to review your MAP and to identify which marriage values need attention.

3. Schedule these marriage-building activities and ideas into your date book organizer, sometimes even on a specific day or even hour and minute. This builds urgency into the activity. This doesn't mean you lose spontaneity. It means you value your marriage relationship enough to make sure that lower-priority activities don't sneak into your life and rob you of the precious time you choose to spend with your spouse.

CHAPTER 7

Where and When

Marriage is not something to be indifferently treated or abused, or something that simply takes care of itself... All things need attention, care and concern, and especially so in this most sensitive of all relationships of life.
—*Richard L. Evans*

You could develop your MAP by sitting down together and working at your kitchen table. We suggest, however, that the quality of your MAP could be enhanced if you plan a special physical setting that will lend itself to kindling feelings of love and commitment. Here are some ideas to help you plan the physical arrangements for developing your MAP:

1. Plan a retreat. Select a weekend when you can spend Friday night (and maybe Saturday night also) away from home. If possible, leave work early on Friday afternoon. Plan well enough so you will not be worried about your business, your children, or any other activity. In fact, forget that you have a business or children. For the next day or so, the total reason you exist is to improve your marriage. Remember, this could be one of the most important experiences of your life. It will be worth the effort, time and expense.

2. Make reservations at a nice hotel—as nice as you can afford. The more "honeymoon-like" the setting, the better. Perhaps a hotel at the beach or in the mountains.

3. Enjoy the drive to the hotel. Check in and become settled in your room. If you arrive early enough, enjoy the pool, hot tub, view, etc. Enjoy each other's company. Make sure that all conversation is uplifting and positive.

4. Have a nice, relaxing dinner. Eat early enough so you will have several hours to talk and plan before retiring. Try not to talk about children, home problems, or anything that needs to be repaired. Be careful not to overeat. You don't want your senses to be dulled.

5. Most hotel rooms have a table and two comfortable chairs. Sit down and begin your session together by expressing appreciation to each other. Perhaps do the visualization exercise (described on page 29), where you rekindle the feelings you had for your spouse at the time you were first married. Just make sure it's positive. Do not dwell to any degree on past shortcomings. This entire experience is about the future—about becoming, building and improving.

6. Begin to build your MAP. Use Chapter 4 and Appendix A of this book as a guide as you begin to identify and define your marriage values. Discuss freely and openly. Listen to your spouse with the purpose of understanding. Realize that you may not agree with some of your spouse's ideas or suggestions. Be sensitive. Remember, differences can be strengths to your marriage if you have the same values. Negotiate—but mostly give. Building your MAP may take several hours, or more, depending on the depth of your discussion.

7. Back to the hot tub. Relax. Have a frozen yogurt or order a snack from room service. Far be it for us to suggest what you do for the rest of the evening.

8. Saturday morning: Sleep in! Arise to a leisurely shower, swim, breakfast or whatever. If you need to check out of

your hotel at noon, plan to spend at least another hour refining your values and discussing goals. Solidify plans for how and when certain values and goals will manifest themselves as actions. Schedule your weekly planning meetings in your date book for the coming month.

When Will You Begin?

It is human nature to resist change, even when the anticipated change would be beneficial for us.

Can you visualize the potential value in building your MAP? Someone who reads this book might say, "I can see the positive impact that these ideas could have on my marriage, but this is a real busy month," or "It's so close to the holidays," or "We'll wait until school starts," or "We'll wait until our children are a little older," etc. When can you possibly find the time to build your MAP? You will probably never find the time, but you can make the time. NOW! Do it now! Sit down now with your spouse. Select a coming weekend and block it off your calendar, just as if it were an important business meeting—which it is. Make reservations at the hotel. Begin making whatever arrangements are necessary to ensure that you will share this experience as soon as possible. It will probably not become easier if you wait.

It has been said that the tragedy of life is not that it ends so soon, but that we wait so long to begin it. Perhaps the same could be said for marriage. Build your MAP now so that two or ten or twenty years from now you can look back on this moment in time and say, "That was a moment that really mattered."

CHAPTER 8

The Challenge of Change

We are, all of us, a reflection of what we do with time, of what we want—or at least what we want enough to be willing to work for.
—*Richard L. Evans*

Now that you have decided to make more time for your marriage, how can you implement these ideas?

Visualization and Planning

During your reading, you have probably mentally pictured yourself doing many things that would enhance your marriage. This visualization is the beginning of behavior change. This is the reason we write values and goals as affirmations. We need to actually see ourselves doing what must be done to earn a happy, successful marriage. Formal planning transfers the visualization from our minds to our specific goals, and finally to our daily "to do" lists.

Performance

Remember that love is not a noun. Love is an action verb. You must do, express, act, share and show. Practice correct marriage principles. Allocate the time, money and other resources necessary for your success.

Page 72

Evaluation

Monitor your progress. Communicate often regarding the strengths and challenges of your marital relationship.

Educational research suggests that if you do not act on new information within 48 hours, you probably won't act on it. Therefore, we challenge you to accept the following assignment. On a piece of paper, write goals stating that you will:

1. Within the next seven days, schedule a specific date and make physical arrangements to complete your MAP.

2. Complete your MAP within 30 days from today.

3. After completing your MAP, hold a marriage planning meeting each week for at least three consecutive weeks. During these weekly meetings, review each other's upcoming schedules, read your MAP, and schedule specific marriage-enhancement activities in your date book organizer or calendar.

Educational research indicates that it takes at least twenty-one days to form a new habit. Don't be discouraged if improvement comes more slowly than you would like. It is possible that your marriage has received little attention for years. Begin by visualizing your ideal marriage relationship. Practice correct marriage principles. Remember, you generally get what you expect and what you're willing to work for.

CHAPTER 9

Family Values

We have been so anxious to give our children what we didn't have that we have neglected to give them what we did have.
—Author unknown

The trouble with being a parent is that by the time you are experienced, you are usually unemployed.
—Author unknown

The value identification process described in Chapter 4 can also be applied in a family setting. We have found it challenging to allocate from our busy schedules the time necessary to provide a stable family environment. Yet one of our highest priorities is to teach our values to our children. This requires spending time with our children talking, playing, helping, vacationing, reading, etc.

We recently held a family meeting for the purpose of identifying our family values. This meeting was attended by us and our five children, ranging in age from 6 to 17. We sat together around the dining room table. We introduced the meeting's purpose by briefly sharing with our children some of our personal and marriage values. We discussed with our children our feeling that having family values would help us improve our family relationships. We then asked for their participation and input in formulating our family value statements.

We listed on a white board the following general family value categories: Intellectual, Physical, Social, Responsibilities and Spiritual. We defined each category, and then, taking each value separately, asked, "What can we do, as a family, to help each of us grow in this area?"

The older children participated more than the younger ones, but everyone contributed and felt like part of the process. We wrote down each suggestion. After we had built a good list, we refined and reworded the value statements as affirmations. We then presented these "family values" to our children, with a brief discussion to make sure that each value was understood. Each family member committed to live by our family values. Using calligraphy, Barbara wrote these family values on heavy paper and posted them on our refrigerator door. They are colorful, attractive and easy to read.

Here are a few examples of our family values from each of the value categories. We share these to give you some ideas for your own family's values. Your value statements will be unique as they reflect your family goals, interests, children's ages, etc.

FAMILY VALUES (General Statement)

We are proud of our family name and keep it honorable.

Intellectual

We strive for excellence in school work and grades.

We do our homework before seeking entertainment.

We limit our TV/computer use.

We read often.

We go to the library at least twice per month.

Physical

We eat well-balanced, nutritious meals.

We limit our eating of fats and sweets.

We get to bed on time every night.

We practice good personal hygiene.

Responsibility

We accept responsibility for our actions.

We take pride in a well-kept home.

We keep our own bedrooms clean.

We complete our daily chores well and on time.

Social

We love each other.

We speak positively to and about each other.

We enjoy family activities, games, outings and vacations.

Spiritual

We have family prayer every day.

We are attentive and we participate in our church meetings.

As you can see, our family values are written as affirmations (statements of ideal behavior). Although we have not achieved all of them yet, they give our family stability and direction.

Each day, we choose a different value category to read together as a family. This is done immediately before dinner, which happens to be one time each day when we are usually all together. This is also when we have our daily family prayer. Each family member is assigned a day of the week. He or she is responsible to select a value category and to read all the value statements in that category. As each value statement is read, the person reading asks, "Is our family doing this?" or "When was the last time we did this?" or "When should we do this next?"

We must confess that our children are fairly normal and are not always ecstatic about this process. We continue to work patiently with them, however, for we believe that the rewards far outweigh the effort.

These value statements have become helpful in matters of family discipline. If there appears to be an infraction of our family values (such as arguing, prolonged TV watching, junk food binges, etc.), rather than yelling or resorting to extreme parental discipline or confrontation, we simply remove our value statements from the refrigerator door and ask the guilty person or persons to read the appropriate value statements (which he or she has agreed to support). This does not always bring a quick and quiet conclusion to the situation, but we have found it much more effective than the more traditional parent/child confrontations.

You may want to make this value identification process a special, unique experience for your family by following the suggestions outlined in Chapter 6. Take your family on a retreat. Spend a night or two at a beach motel or a nice campground. Pools, hot tubs, fun activities, sun tanning, amusement parks, hiking, etc. help create an atmosphere conducive to total family participation in this process. After they've agreed to support their family values, they shouldn't complain if you point out that they have just broken one of "their" family values.

Our family values have made a positive contribution to the quality of our family life. We hope these ideas will be helpful to you and your family. We truly believe that the best thing you can spend on your children is your time.

APPENDIX A

MAP-Building Steps

Step 1. Identify marriage value categories. Select from the following general categories:

Children/Family

Cultural

Extended family

Financial

Hobbies

Humanitarian

Intellectual/Educational

Personal fulfillment

Physical

Political

Social

Spiritual

Work/Job/Professional

Step 2. Write statements describing ideal behavior (affirmations) supporting each value (see example on facing page). Use the forms on the following pages to guide you through these first two MAP-building steps.

Financial

MAP Value Category

Affirmations supporting this value:

1. We prepare and follow a family budget.
2. We agree before making major purchases.
3. We earn more money than we spend.
4. We save for future known and unknown expenses.

MAP Value Category

Affirmations supporting this value:

_____

_____

_____

_____

_____

_____

_____

_____

_____

_____

_____

_____

_____

MAP Value Category

Affirmations supporting this value:

_____

_____

_____

_____

_____

_____

_____

_____

_____

_____

_____

_____

_____

_____

_____

MAP Value Category

Affirmations supporting this value:

_____

_____

_____

_____

_____

_____

_____

_____

_____

_____

_____

_____

_____

_____

MAP Value Category

Affirmations supporting this value:

_____

_____

_____

_____

_____

_____

_____

_____

_____

_____

_____

_____

_____

_____

_____

MAP Value Category

Affirmations supporting this value:

_____

_____

_____

_____

_____

_____

_____

_____

_____

_____

_____

_____

_____

_____

_____

MAP Value Category

Affirmations supporting this value:

_____

_____

_____

_____

_____

_____

_____

_____

_____

_____

_____

_____

_____

_____

MAP Value Category

Affirmations supporting this value:

_____

_____

_____

_____

_____

_____

_____

_____

_____

_____

_____

_____

_____

_____

_____

MAP Value Category

Affirmations supporting this value:

_____

_____

_____

_____

_____

_____

_____

_____

_____

_____

_____

_____

_____

_____

_____

MAP Goal-Planning

You are now ready to set goals based on your marriage values. Goal setting is the process whereby you bring your behavior (reality) in line with your value statements (ideals).

For detailed instructions on goal setting, see pages 55 through 59 in chapter 5.

Remember to use the S. M. A. R. T. method to make your goal setting more effective:

S - Specific

M - Measurable

A - Attainable

R - Realistic

T - Time-scheduled

Use the examples and forms on the following pages to guide your MAP goal-setting.

MAP Goal-Planning

Long-term Goal:
(Specific, Measurable, Attainable, Realistic, Time-scheduled)
One year from today (Jan. 2), we will be out of debt, and we will be saving at least #200 per month.

Short-term Goals:	Target Date	Date Completed
1. We review our bank statement and budget by the 10th each month.	Jan. 10	
2. We have stopped using our credit cards.	Jan. 2	
3. We pay an extra #200 p. month to pay off our credit card.	paid-off May 1	
4. We will not purchase any new clothes for 3 months.	Mar. 31	
5. We save #50 p. month in a separate savings acct.	Mar. 31	
6. We save #100 p. month.	June 30	

MAP Goal-Planning

Long-term Goal: (Specific, Measurable, Attainable, Realistic, Time-scheduled)

Short-term Goals:	Target Date	Date Completed
1.		
2.		
3.		
4.		
5.		
6.		

MAP Goal-Planning

Long-term Goal: (Specific, Measurable, Attainable, Realistic, Time-scheduled)

Short-term Goals:	Target Date	Date Completed
1.		
2.		
3.		
4.		
5.		
6.		

MAP Goal-Planning

Long-term Goal:
(Specific, Measurable, Attainable, Realistic, Time-scheduled)

Short-term Goals:	Target Date	Date Completed
1.		
2.		
3.		
4.		
5.		
6.		

MAP Goal-Planning

Long-term Goal: (Specific, Measurable, Attainable, Realistic, Time-scheduled)

Short-term Goals:	Target Date	Date Completed
1.		
2.		
3.		
4.		
5.		
6.		

MAP Goal-Planning

Long-term Goal: (Specific, Measurable, Attainable, Realistic, Time-scheduled)

Short-term Goals:	Target Date	Date Completed
1.		
2.		
3.		
4.		
5.		
6.		

MAP Goal-Planning

Long-term Goal: (Specific, Measurable, Attainable, Realistic, Time-scheduled)

Short-term Goals:	Target Date	Date Completed
1.		
2.		
3.		
4.		
5.		
6.		

MAP Goal-Planning

Long-term Goal: (Specific, Measurable, Attainable, Realistic, Time-scheduled)

Short-term Goals:	Target Date	Date Completed
1.		
2.		
3.		
4.		
5.		
6.		

MAP Goal-Planning

Long-term Goal:
(Specific, Measurable, Attainable, Realistic, Time-scheduled)

Short-term Goals:	Target Date	Date Completed
1.		
2.		
3.		
4.		
5.		
6.		

APPENDIX B

The Date Book Organizer

A date book organizer can help you maintain control and stay organized. Your date book becomes your tool to apply the time management principles described in this book. Date books come in various sizes, prices and degrees of complexity. They are even available as electronic devices or computer programs. We share the following ideas for consideration as you begin to upgrade or select a date book organizer:

1. **A daily appointment schedule.** Make sure you have enough room to write commitments you make both inside and outside of the typical 8 to 5 workday. Most of your marriage commitments will not occur between 8 am and 5 pm.

2. **A daily "To Do" list.** There should be a place to prioritize your daily tasks as well as a place to check off completed tasks. Some people prefer to organize from a weekly schedule. This does provide the advantage to visually plan ahead and anticipate more easily.

3. **Space for notes.** You should have space to write daily notes, lists, thoughts, journal entries, etc.

4. **A place for your value, goal, and affirmation statements.** Your MAP statements should be in your date book organizer so you can have easy access to them whenever you want. You will find little unexpected gifts of free time when you're waiting in a doctor's or dentist's office, waiting in line or for a meeting to begin, riding the bus or waiting for a plane. Review your MAP during

these times. As you read, ask yourself, "When was the last time I did something about that marriage value?" "Isn't it about time we do that again?" etc. We're sure you can see the benefit of always having your date book with you.

5. **Flexibility.** Customize your date book organizer to meet your needs. You can add family pictures, address/phone directories, calculators, credit card holders, check book registers, etc., to the extent these additions would be helpful to you.

Regardless of the organizational tool you select, make sure it meets your needs. Some couples have found it beneficial for both spouses to use the same date book system.

APPENDIX C

Inspirational Thoughts Relating to Time and Marriage

The future is the time when you'll wish you'd done what you aren't doing now.
                                    —Author Unknown

Time is a great teacher, but unfortunately it kills all its pupils.
                                    —Hector Berlioz

What would be the use of immortality to a person who cannot use well a half hour?
                                    —Ralph Waldo Emerson

*The clock of life is wound but once
and no man has the power
To tell just when the hands will stop
at late or early hour.
Now is the only time you own.
Live, love, toil with a will.
Place no faith in tomorrow,
for the clock may then be still.*
                                    —F. B. Meyer

He who marries for money earns it.
                                    —Confucious

Before you marry, keep your two eyes open; after you marry, shut one.
—Jamaican Proverb

A truly happy marriage is one in which a woman gives the best years of her life to the man who made them the best. *—Author Unknown*

The thing that counts most in the pursuit of happiness is choosing the right traveling companion.
—Adrian Anderson

Two shall be born the whole wide world apart
And bend each wandering step to this one end
That, one day, out of darkness they shall meet
And read life's meaning in each other's eyes.
—Susan Marr Spaulding

The marriages we regard as the happiest are those in which each of the partners believes that he or she got the best deal.
—Author Unknown

As long as I was fortunate enough to have a wife, I had adopted the habit of letting myself be guided by her opinion on difficult matters, for women, I believe, have a certain feel, which is more reliable than our reasonings.
—Benjamin Franklin

Whatever woman may cast her lot with mine, should any ever do so, it is my intention to do all in my power to make her happy and contented; and there is nothing I can imagine that would make me more unhappy than to fail in the effort.
                    —Abraham Lincoln

Too often we love things and use people when we should be using things and loving people.
                    —Author Unknown

It's good to have money and the things that money can buy, but it's good, too, to check up once in a while and make sure you haven't lost the things that money can't buy.
                    —George Horace Lorimer

Our responsibility is not discharged by the announcement of virtuous ends.
                    —John F. Kennedy

We are most of us very lonely in this world; you who have any who love you, cling to them and thank God.
                    —Author Unknown

The past is to learn from and not to live in.
                    —Richard L. Evans

In most quarrels there is a fault on both sides. A quarrel may be compared to a spark, which cannot be produced without a flint as well as steel.
—Charles Caleb Colton

The real art of conversation is not only to say the right thing at the right place but to leave unsaid the wrong thing at the tempting moment.
—Dorothy Nevill

To keep your marriage brimming
With love in the loving cup,
Whenever you're wrong, admit it.
Whenever you're right, shut up.
—Ogden Nash

I will speak ill of no man, not even in matters of truth; but rather excuse the faults I hear charged upon others, and upon proper occasion speak all the good I know of everybody.
—Benjamin Franklin

I have yet to find a man, whatever his situation in life, who did not do better work and put forth greater effort under a spirit of approval than he ever would do under a spirit of criticism.
—Charles M. Schwab

The greater the man, the greater the courtesy.
—Alfred Lord Tennyson

Marriage should be a duet—when one sings, the other claps.
                    —Joe Murray

Love does not consist in gazing at each other but in looking together in the same direction.
                    —Antoine De Saint-exupery

We have been told that "when a man retires, it is nice if he has a hobby that his wife can share with him—like if her favorite pastime is cleaning fish."

We are also aware of a woman who said to her friend, "I got a set of golf clubs for my husband." Her friend's reply: "Gee, I wonder how much I could get for my husband."

Notes:

Notes:

Notes:

MAP Follow-up

We would like you to share with us the results of your MAP-building experience. After using your MAP as a marriage guide for at least one month, please write a brief letter to us reporting your results. We want to know if your MAP-building experience is as positive as ours has been.

Mail your letter to the following address:

Bryce and Barbara Winkel
2465 N.W. 145th Ave.
Beaverton, Oregon 97006

Isn't It About Time for Your Marriage? is also available as a seminar. The seminar curriculum adapts easily for presentation to business, educational or religious groups. If interested, please write to us at the above address.

About the Authors

Bryce and Barbara Winkel have gained the experience to write this book through their nineteen years of marriage. Barbara enjoys her role as mother to their five children. She is an accomplished pianist and practices dental hygiene on a part-time basis. She was recently named Oregon Young Mother Representative.

Bryce is a seasoned professional educator with a doctoral degree in education. He is an entertaining and popular speaker to both youth and adult age groups. He teaches time management, money management and marriage enrichment seminars.

The Winkels live in Beaverton, Oregon.